RYA Powerboat Scheme Syllabus & Logbook

First published 2004
Second edition 2013
Revised and updated August 2013
Reprinted March 2014
Reprinted August 2014
Updated May 2015
Reprinted February 2016
Reprinted September 2016
Reprinted March 2017
Reprinted August 2017
Reprinted March 2018
Reprinted August 2018

Published by
The Royal Yachting Association
RYA House, Ensign Way, Hamble,
Southampton, SO31 4YA
Tel: 02380 604 100
Web: www.rya.org.uk
Follow us on Twitter @RYAPublications or on YouTube

We welcome feedback on our publications at publications@rya.org.uk

You can check content updates for RYA publications at www.rya.org.uk/go/bookschangelog

© 2013 Royal Yachting Association

RYA Order Code: G20
ISBN: 978-1-906435882
Photo credits: Paul Glatzel, Adam Wilson, Chris Floyd
Cover photo: Paul Wyeth
Printed in China through World Print Ltd.

FOREWORD

Welcome to the exciting sport of powerboating. The RYA Powerboat Scheme meets the training needs of recreational and professional powerboat operators alike. Whether you are an amateur with a keen sense of adventure, or use powerboats as part of your job, the RYA Powerboat Scheme will train you in all aspects of safe boat handling and navigation. Adopted by many countries, RYA powerboat courses remain the most popular in the world.

Rachel Andrews
Chief Instructor, Motor Cruising & Power

Maritime and Coastguard Agency

This MCA logo denotes certificates which can be endorsed for commercial use. For more details and an application form for a commercial endorsement, please visit the RYA website.

CONTENTS

This book is effective for courses from 1 January 2013

1 INTRODUCTION

RYA Training

One of the strengths of the RYA is its training schemes for all aspects of boating, from windsurfing to offshore cruising. The principle underlying each of these schemes is Education rather than Legislation, because we believe that a higher standard of competence can be achieved by voluntary training rather than by legislation requiring registration and driver licensing. You can support this principle by your involvement in the RYA Powerboat Scheme.

The courses described in this publication are run at RYA Recognised Training Centres around the world. RYA recognition is your safeguard, ensuring that you will be taught by experienced, qualified instructors in suitable, seaworthy boats, to the syllabus given.

Before a powerboating school, club or centre can gain RYA recognition it is inspected to ensure that certain minimum standards are met. Regular and spot inspections ensure that these same standards are maintained.

For full details of RYA recognition, instructor training and a list of centres visit the RYA's website *www.rya.org.uk*.

Other Water Users

If you are the driver of a powerboat you have a great responsibility towards other water users. The RYA Powerboat Scheme has been developed to advise you of that responsibility at the same time as training you to handle your boat in a seamanlike manner, so that you and your passengers can all enjoy being afloat.

Powerboat drivers sometimes attract publicity, often through lack of awareness of the basic rules and customs of the sea. You can help to redress the balance through courteous driving and by displaying a skilful approach to boat handling.

RYA Membership

If you are not already a member of the RYA, we would be delighted to welcome you aboard. We deal with all aspects of boating and have a lot to offer.
You'll find more details on page 48 of this book.

Powerboating Abroad

Many countries require the owners or drivers of powerboats to hold a certificate of competence, even if only visiting the country for a holiday. To meet this requirement, the RYA issues the International Certificate of Competence, which you will need if you intend to take your boat abroad. The RYA Level 2 Powerboat Handling Certificate is the standard required. Contact one of our Training Centres or visit *www.rya.org.uk*.

Powerboaters with Special Needs

Recognising that some powerboaters with disabilities are unable to complete the full requirements for an RYA course completion certificate without additional help, the scheme makes provision for the logbook to be endorsed as appropriate. The endorsement will indicate the sections of the syllabus for which the powerboater requires assistance.

The RYA Powerboat Scheme is applicable to sportsboats, RIBs, dories and launches, and other boats which do not normally provide accommodation or cooking facilities. Training on boats with accommodation is covered by the RYA Motor Cruising Scheme explained in logbook G158 RYA Yachtmaster Scheme Syllabus & Logbook. The lower age limit for RYA powerboat courses is 8 years old, but the RYA would not recommend under 16s being left in charge of a powerboat without adult supervision.

Full details of the scheme are given in this handbook:

Level 1 Start Powerboating	Provides a practical introduction to boat handling skills.
Level 2 Powerboat Handling	Provides the skills and background knowledge needed by the competent powerboat driver and is the basis of the International Certificate of Competence.
Powerboat Tender Operators	Covers navigation for short ship-to-shore transfers by day and night and considerations for dealing with guests on board.
Intermediate Day Cruising	Covers practical use of pilotage and passage planning by day on coastal waters, using a wide variety of navigational techniques.
Advanced Day & Night	Provides the skills and background knowledge needed by powerboat drivers operating by day or night in known or unfamiliar waters, the skipper's role and boat handling in more demanding conditions.
Safety Boat	Provides the skills required when acting as an escort craft, safety boat or coach boat for a fleet of dinghies, windsurfers or canoes and for racing or training activities.

The Syllabi

The following pages describe the syllabus for each level of the RYA Powerboat Scheme. Due to time constraints and variations in course locations and equipment, not all subjects can be covered in great detail or practically on the water. We have therefore specified three levels of teaching to show you in how much depth you can expect each item to be covered. These three levels are:

KNOWLEDGE of the subject
The subject will be briefly explained. Familiarisation during the course and information on where to find out more.

UNDERSTANDS the subject
The subject will be covered in greater depth. You will be asked to demonstrate a basic understanding and go away from the course able to develop further your own skill in this area. Confirmation of your understanding of the subject may be achieved in a number of ways during the course.

CAN demonstrate a level of proficiency in the subject
The subject will be covered in great depth, including background theory, practical demonstrations by the instructor and repeated practice by yourself until you can demonstrate good skills in this subject.

The course structures are shown on the next two pages.

LEVEL 1 START POWERBOATING
Preparation
- Launching and recovering
- Safety equipment
- Pre-start checks
- Personal buoyancy

Boat Handling and Manoeuvres
- Starting and stopping
- Use of killcord
- Steering controls
- Securing to a buoy
- Leaving and coming alongside
- Being towed

Theory and Background
- IRPCS
- Ropework
- Awareness of other water users
- Man overboard

LEVEL 2 POWERBOAT HANDLING
Preparation
- Launching and recovering
- Safety equipment
- Lines and fenders
- Fuel tanks

Boat Handling and Manoeuvres
- Effects of current or tide
- Planing and low speed manoeuvring
- Propeller controls
- Securing to a buoy
- Anchoring
- Leaving and coming alongside
- Man overboard

Theory and Background
- Types of craft and engine
- Maintenance checks
- IRPCS
- Weather forecasts
- Emergency action

SAFETY BOAT
Preparation
- Safety equipment
- Assistance with race management
- Crew communication

Boat Handling and Manoeuvres
- Positioning in respect to fleet
- Standing off another craft
- Coming alongside under way
- Dinghy (including high performance) and windsurfer rescue
- Towing
- Mark laying

Theory and Background
- Rescue of other water users
- Communication
- VHF
- First aid

Maritime and Coastguard Agency

POWERBOAT TENDER OPERATOR

Preparation
- Life-saving appliances
- Passenger safety and comfort
- Daytime pilotage

Boat Handling & Manoeuvres
- Berthing single-handed
- Night pilotage using electronic navigational aids
- Emergency situations

INTERMEDIATE POWERBOAT DAY CRUISING

Preparation
- Pilotage
- Navigation
- Fuel and engine checks

Boat Handling and Manoeuvres
- Effect of waves and rougher conditions
- Power trim and trim tabs
- Berthing in differing situations
- Use of GPS in planning navigation and pilotage by day
- It is strongly recommended that candidates hold a first aid certificate and a VHF operator's certificate.

ADVANCED POWERBOAT DAY AND NIGHT

Preparation
- Passage planning
- Meteorology
- Skipper's responsibilities

Boat Handling and Manoeuvres
- Planing boat handling
- Advanced manoeuvres
- Manoeuvring in rough weather
- Chart plotters and radar
- Pilotage by day and night
- Emergency situations
- Differences for a twin-engine vessel
- It is strongly recommended that candidates hold a first aid certificate and a VHF operator's certificate.

RYA/MCA ADVANCED POWERBOAT CERTIFICATE OF COMPETENCE

Maritime and Coastguard Agency

Pre-exam Experience:
- Two years' relevant experience including night pilotage.
- As a guide: 30 days, 2 days as skipper, 800 miles, 12 night hours.

For Holders of the Advanced Powerboat Course Completion Certificate:
- Twenty days, 2 days as skipper, 400 miles, 12 night hours.

Form of Examination:
- Practical exam lasting 4–5 hours for one candidate, up to 7 hours for 2 or 3 candidates.

Certification Required before Examination:
- VHF/SRC Operator's licence
- First aid certificate

YOUR POWERBOAT CHECK LIST

Tell someone where you are going and when you plan to return, and inform them when you have returned.

Listen to the weather forecast

If in doubt, don't go out

Before going afloat check:

Personal and boat buoyancy

Alternative means of propulsion

Anchor, chain and warp

Bucket, bailer or bilge pump

Fuel, including reserve tank

First aid kit

Sharp knife

Engine emergency spares

Fire extinguisher

Flares as appropriate

VHF radio

Compass, electronic aids and charts when necessary

Car and trailer are properly parked

When afloat:

Keep a good look-out at all times

Don't overload your boat

Obey speed limits in harbours/estuaries etc.

Keep to the right in rivers/narrow channels

When crossing a channel, cross quickly at right angles

Keep clear of swimmers, fishermen, canoeists, dinghy sailors, windsurfers and boats/small buoys flying Code Flag A ('I have a diver down')

Think how your wash will affect others

Look out for deteriorating weather conditions

On the road:

Secure boat to trailer and stow all loose gear

Cover your propeller with a prop bag

Trailer lights must repeat those on the rear of the car, including a rear fog light if fitted to the car

Allow extra braking distance if your trailer is unbraked

Corner and reverse with care

Park your car and trailer clear of slipways and above the high-water mark

Use the correct number plate

Aim: To provide a practical introduction to boat handling and safety in powerboats. The course may be conducted in a variety of boat types, both planing and displacement, and the certificate issued will be endorsed to show the type of boat in which the training took place. The ratio of students to instructors should not exceed 3:1.

Duration: One day

Minimum age: Eight years old

Endorsements: Is aged 8–11 years and therefore should only use powered craft under the supervision of a responsible adult on board the craft

Is aged 12–15 years and therefore the holder should only use powered craft under the supervision of a responsible adult

Assistance required to complete the course

Section A: Practical Boat Handling
Launch and Recovery (8 to 11-year-olds to observe this session only)
Knowledge of:
- Considerations to be taken during the launch
- The use of a trailer or launching trolley
- Considerations to be taken regarding sea conditions and hazards
- Construction, width and condition of ramp/slipway

Preparation of Boat and Crew
Understands:
- Personal buoyancy and appropriate clothing
- The use of the following equipment: lines, fenders, anchor and warp, bailer, fire extinguisher, pump, paddles or oars, compass, flares, torch, whistle, charts, first aid kit, sharp knife.

Can:
- Perform the following: fasten to a cleat and stow an anchor

Boat Handling
Knowledge of:
- Planing boats: propeller angle and immersion, use of shallow drive
- Low-speed handling: ahead and astern
- Displacement boats: handling ahead and astern, carrying way in neutral

(Continued overleaf)

Understands:

- How to carry out pre-start checks, including fuel tank and fuel bulb
- Steering, controls and windage

Can:

- Steer and control boat speed
- Start and stop the engine
- Demonstrate the use of an appropriate length killcord at all times

Picking up and Securing to a Mooring Buoy
Knowledge of:

- Preparation of mooring warps
- Use of a boat hook
- Method of approach
- Crew communication
- Making fast

Leaving and Coming Alongside
Knowledge of:

- Wind effect
- Approach in tidal stream or current

Understands:

- Leaving – ahead or astern

Can:

- Demonstrate the use of painter, lines and fenders, attachment to boat, stowage under way
- Control speed and angle of approach
- Make fast alongside

Section B: Theory

Knowledge of:

- Loading and balancing the boat and the effect on handling and performance
- Local byelaws and insurance

Understands:

- Crew numbers: minimum number in the boat, keeping a look-out
- Awareness of other water users, including effect of wash
- Application of IRPCS. Understands rules 5, 6, and conduct around commercial shipping in confined waters

Man Overboard
Understands:

- How to stop the boat
- Raising the alarm
- Prevention

Essential Navigation and Seamanship

This course is great for those who have just completed their RYA Powerboat Level 2 or are preparing for a Powerboat Instructor Course and are looking to cruise locally in daylight.

Available online and in the classroom, this course gives you the essential knowledge needed when you're afloat. The topics include:

- Charts and publications
- Engine checks
- Tidal awareness
- Pilotage
- Anchoring
- Passage planning

- Safety
- Buoyage
- Visual and electronic navigation
- Rules of the road
- Weather forecasts

You will receive a course pack which includes a chart, plotter, dividers, course handbook, exercises and an electronic chart plotter CD.

How long is the course?
In the classroom, the course is taught over 16 hours with exercises to complete along the way. It can be covered as a series of short sessions or over two full days. Online, the course will take around six hours, but the beauty of it is that you can work through it at your own speed, whenever and wherever you like.

Taking the course online
Our online Essential Navigation and Seamanship course is run through recognised training centres using the RYA Interactive website. You can see more information and a 'taster' here: *www.ryainteractive.org.*

RYA Interactive courses can be taken any time, anywhere and at your own speed. All you need is a computer and the internet.

Maritime and Coastguard Agency

Aim: To teach boat handling and seamanship in powerboats. The course may be conducted in a variety of boat types, both planing and displacement, and the certificate issued will be endorsed to show the type of boat in which the training took place. The ratio of students to instructors should not exceed 3:1.

Duration: Two days

Minimum age: Twelve years old

Endorsement: Is aged 12–15 and therefore the holder should only use powered craft under the supervision of a responsible adult

Assistance required to complete the course

Section A: Practical
Launching and Recovery
Knowledge of:

- Use of a trailer or launching trolley
- Consideration of launching and sea conditions, including hazards and obstructions
- Number of persons required to launch/recover
- Construction, width and condition of slipway
- Steep/slippery slipways, beach launching, lee shores
- Care of trailer bearings, hitch, lashings, ties, lights and winch
- Trailer parking

Can:

- Prepare the boat, lines, fenders, safety equipment, fuel tanks, lines and secure gear on board
- Prepare to go afloat
- Tie relevant knots

Preparation of Boat and Crew
Understands:

- Personal buoyancy and appropriate clothing
- The use of the following equipment: lines, fenders, anchor and warp, bailer, fire extinguisher, pump, paddles or oars, compass, flares, torch, whistle, charts, first aid kit, sharp knife

Boat Handling
Knowledge of:

- Loading: effect on handling and performance, effect on balance and trim, CE Plate and manufacturer's recommendation
- Handling characteristics of displacement boats, rudder-steered craft and shaft-driven vessels

(Continued overleaf)

4 LEVEL 2 POWERBOAT HANDLING

Understands:
- Crew members: minimum number in faster craft, keeping a look-out
- The importance of boat control in waves and adequate seating to minimise the possibility of injury
- Awareness of other water users, including effect of wash
- Steering, controls, effect of current or tidal stream
- Handling a boat at planing speed, trim tabs and power trim
- Planing boats: propeller angle and immersion, shallow drive, planing and displacement speed handling, tiller/console steering

Can:
- Carry out pre-start checks, engine starting and stopping
- Demonstrate the use of an appropriate length killcord at all times
- Carry out low speed manoeuvres including: turning in a confined area, effect of wind on bow and holding off. Demonstrate an awareness of the danger of flooding when going astern
- Handle a boat at planing speed

Securing to a Buoy

Understands:
- Preparation of mooring warp
- Use of a boat hook
- Direction of approach
- Taking way off
- Crew communication
- Making fast
- Procedure when overshooting

Can:
- Approach and secure to buoy

Anchoring

Knowledge of:
- Types of anchor
- Stowage and attachment to boat
- Preparation of anchor, chain and warp
- Weighing anchor

Understands:
- Correct approach in various conditions
- Taking way off
- Crew communication
- Check holding
- Depth of water, holding ground, scope required

Can:
- Approach and anchor correctly
- Weigh anchor correctly

Leaving and Coming Alongside
Understands:
- Preparation and use of lines and fenders, attachment to boat, stowage under way
- Speed and angle of approach
- Wind effect
- Method of approach in tidal stream or current

Can:
- Make fast alongside
- Use springs
- Leave – ahead or astern

Man Overboard
Knowledge of:
- Recovery of man overboard

Understands:
- Cold shock
- How and when to raise the alarm

Can:
- Take immediate action
- Observe the man overboard
- Carry out the correct return with awareness of propeller
- Approach and recover the 'man' in the water. (Small weighted buoy to be used)
- Demonstrate both drift down and into wind approach method
- Switch engine off

Section B: Theory
Knowledge of:
- Types of craft: advantages and disadvantages of different hull forms with respect to sea-keeping ability
- Seating arrangements
- Stepped hulls

(Continued overleaf)

4 | LEVEL 2 POWERBOAT HANDLING

- Engines and drives: advantages and disadvantages of outboard, inboard and outdrive units, single and twin-shaft drives, choice and use of fuels
- Siting of fuel tanks, fuel lines, batteries, wiring, fire extinguishers
- Routine engine maintenance checks, basic fault diagnosis
- Close down procedure
- Advice to inland drivers about coastal waters
- Use and limitations of GPS/chart plotters
- Application of local byelaws, especially around commercial shipping
- Sources of weather information

Understands:
- Awareness of other water users
- Communication with other craft
- Disabled craft
- Emergency action, preventing sinking
- Adrift – alternative means of propulsion
- Actions to be taken by a disabled craft and being towed
- Fire precautions and fire fighting
- Distress signals, means of issuing distress, DSC and the Mayday call
- Advice for vessels in restricted visibility

Can:
- Apply IRPCS, principally rules 5, 6, 7, 8, 9, 12–18

Section C: Coastal

Knowledge of:
- Byelaws and local regulations
- Insurance
- Boat registration schemes

Understands:
- Pilotage and passage planning
- Charts, chart symbols, buoyage systems
- Tides and tidal streams

Can:
- Use steering and hand-bearing compasses
- Apply Section A on coastal waters

Section D: Direct Assessment for Experienced Powerboat Drivers

The candidate should have the equivalent of at least one full season's powerboat-handling experience.

The candidate must complete the practical exercise described overleaf, and satisfactorily answer questions on Section B.

Candidates seeking assessment on coastal waters will demonstrate a knowledge and practical application of Section C.

Practical Assessment of all Candidates for Level 2

The practical exercise detailed in the diagram overleaf shows the manoeuvres required to be demonstrated during the practical assessment. Candidates are expected to show that they understand the principles of each manoeuvre. Failure to complete a manoeuvre successfully at the first attempt will not necessarily result in overall failure, but a timely awareness of the need to abort an exercise and try again is important.

(Level 2 test diagram overleaf)

Powerboat Handling Level 2
direct assessment

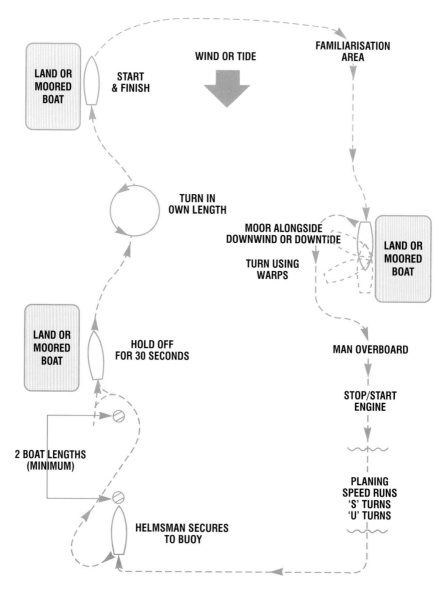

Aim: To introduce the techniques used in powerboats escorting racing fleets of dinghies and windsurfers, providing safety and rescue cover for training fleets, and assisting in race management. Techniques for canoes/kayaks and kite surfers should also be discussed. It is strongly recommended that a member of the rescue crew should hold a first aid certificate (or should have experience of first aid). The ratio of students to instructors should not exceed 6:1 (using two boats).

Eligibility: RYA Level 2 Powerboat Handling

Duration: Two days

Minimum age: Sixteen years old

Endorsement: Assistance required to complete the course

Section A: Practical

Preparation
Understands:
- Boat checks
- Safety equipment including killcord management, sharp knife and first aid kit
- Crew communication
- Race management duties including marking abandoned boats

Boat Handling
Understands:
- Positioning in respect to fleet
- Size of sailing area and response times for different craft
- Communication with other craft
- Race management duties

Can:
- Stand off another craft
- Come alongside under way – sailing craft
- Lay and recover marks
- Demonstrate the correct use of an appropriate-length killcord at all times

Dinghy Rescue
Understands:
- Methods for recovering personnel from water and techniques for lifting heavy casualties
- How to deal with entrapments
- How to right a multihull
- Procedures for righting high-performance dinghies
- The dangers of lee shores

(Continued overleaf)

5 SAFETY BOAT

Can:
- Approach capsized craft and boats in need of assistance
- Right capsized and inverted or partially inverted dinghies, both crewed and single-handers

Windsurfer Rescue
Understands:
- Recovering several boards

Can:
- Demonstrate the correct approach
- Recover personnel from water
- Rescue single board without de-rigging
- Stow rigs

Kayak or Canoe Rescue (can be covered as theory)
Knowledge of:
- The correct approach
- How to rescue different types of kayak and canoe
- How to return the paddler to his kayak or canoe
- How to stow empty kayaks
- Towing occupied and empty kayaks or canoes

Towing
Understands:
- Length of tow line
- Multiple tows
- Towing fragile high-performance boats

Can:
- Tow alongside
- Position to pass a tow line
- Pass a tow line
- Use a bridle
- Cast off a tow

SAFETY BOAT | 5

End-of-day Procedures
Understands:
- Refuelling including risks from static electricity and mobile phones
- Returning equipment
- Reporting faults and problems

Section B: Theory
Safety
Understands:
- Use of VHF
- Use of tower or club race box for improved vision
- First aid
- Operating from a beach or in shallow water

Suitability of Craft
Knowledge of:
- Limitations of craft with high freeboard
- Hull types
- Drive types

Local Factors
Knowledge of:
- Byelaws and regulations

Communication
Understands:
- Crew communication
- Communication with other vessels

Rescuing other Water Users
Knowledge of:
- How to rescue swimmers, rowing (sculling) boats, water-skiers and towed inflatables, personal watercraft and larger craft
- Special considerations for dealing with kite surfers

6 | TENDER OPERATOR

Aim: To teach tender driving up to the required standard to carry passengers and other crew members to and from the mother vessel by day and night.

Pre-course knowledge: Candidates must hold an RYA Powerboat Level 2 with coastal endorsement. It is strongly recommended that candidates hold a valid first aid certificate and a VHF/SRC operator's licence or equivalent.

Duration: Two days

Minimum age: Seventeen years old

Section A: Practical

Preparation for Sea

Can:

Prepare the vessel, including:
* Navigation equipment
* Bilge pump and alarms
* Essential safety equipment
* Stowage of warps and securing gear

Pre-departure Procedures

Understands:
* Drive systems
* Emergency shutdown procedures for the vessel being used for training
* The need to be familiar with procedures for refuelling onboard and at sea
* Communication protocol with mother vessel

Can:

Carry out fuel and mechanical checks on the vessel being used for training, including:
* Engines, cooling and lubrication systems
* Safely starting and shutting down engines
* Diagnosing basic engine-start problems
* Fuel levels

Life-saving Apparatus (LSA)

Knowledge of:
* Sources of information on different types of LSA

Understands:
* The importance of familiarisation with the use of different types of LSA

Can:
* Demonstrate the use of all LSA carried onboard

Boat Handling

Understands:
* The importance of having crew to assist in berthing operations
* The importance of boat control in waves and adequate seating to minimize the possibility of injury

- How to select an anchorage with due regard to the safety of the vessel and passengers who may be partaking in water sports
- Towing water toys and the need for a spotter
- Tidal considerations

Can:
- Demonstrate the correct use of the kill cord at all times when under way
- Demonstrate berthing and docking skills in the following situations: beam to; bow to, and stern to, carried out with a crew member and shorthanded
- Helm considerately at planing speed
- Recover an MOB by day and night
- Anchor the vessel safely

Rules of the Road
Knowledge of:
- Sources of local byelaws

Understands:
- The importance of adhering to local byelaws

Can:
- Apply the International Regulations for Preventing Collisions at Sea (IRPCS)
- Demonstrate a good sense of situational awareness including the ability to conduct dynamic risk assessment given the prevailing conditions and location

Passenger Safety and Comfort
Knowledge of:
- Sources of information regarding maximum number of people and payload

Understands:
- When to instruct passengers to wear appropriate LSA
- The importance of boat control in waves and appropriate seating to minimise the possibility of injury or ejection
- The requirement to comply with maximum number of people and payload
- The hazards associated with non-compliant passengers and those under the influence of alcohol
- The hazards associated with less-mobile passengers and children
- Strategies for ensuring the safety of non-English-speaking passengers
- The importance of selecting a safe place to meet and greet passengers
- The need to pre-plan onward land transportation of passengers

Can:
- Brief the crew on passage plan, roles and responsibilities
- Give an effective passenger-safety briefing
- Give an effective demonstration of all relevant LSA and location
- Embark and disembark passengers safely

(Continued overleaf)

- Drive appropriate to prevailing weather and sea conditions, with due consideration to keeping all onboard comfortable and dry

Daytime Pilotage

Understands:

- The benefit of agreeing and lodging the pilotage plan with the Master or Officer of the Watch
- The requirement for a safety margin when using chart plotters and other electronic navigation aids
- The need to use a secondary means of position fixing when using electronic navigation aids, including the use of verifiable waypoints
- The need for consideration of local environmental conditions, hazards and other water users
- The importance of maintaining contact with the mother vessel at all times
- Safe speed for navigation

Can:

- Produce an effective daytime pilotage plan
- Use charts and publications
- Interpret Lateral and Cardinal buoyage systems A and B
- Use a chart plotter for navigation afloat
- Use waypoint navigation
- Use pilotage to enter a port by day

Night-time Pilotage

Understands:

- The additional hazards associated with moving passengers by water during the hours of darkness

Can:

- Take charge of a power-driven vessel during the hours of darkness, including but not limited to short passages between harbour and mother vessel
- Produce an effective night-time pilotage plan
- Demonstrate ability to keep a proper look-out by all available means
- Identify position at all times

Emergency Situations

Knowledge of:

- Helicopter rescue procedures
- Local safe havens/points of refuge

Understands:
- Effective management of an emergency situation by day and at night
- The importance of keeping an up-to-date headcount of all persons on board
- Fire prevention and fighting
- What action to take in the event of hull damage/loss of watertight integrity
- What to do in a medical emergency
- The principles of towing and being towed
- The danger of cold shock

Can:
- Simulate a distress alert by all available means

Section B: Theory
Types of Tender
Knowledge of:
- Different types of tender
- Different types of propulsion systems: outdrive; outboard; jet drive; forward-facing drives, shaft drive

Understands:
- The handling characteristics for various types of common hull forms

Launch and Recovery
Knowledge of:
- Various methods of launch and recovery from the mother vessel while at anchor and stopped in the water

Understands:
- The requirement to gain onboard type-specific training

Legislation and Guidance
Knowledge of:
- The requirement to maintain a current MCA Officer of the Watch Training Record Book (Yacht)
- RYA code of practice for safe watersports operations
- RYA guidance on passenger safety on small commercial high-speed craft

Understands:
- The importance of carrying the correct documents

Vessel-specific Training
Knowledge of:
- Additional regulated training available

Understands:
- The importance of vessel- and equipment-specific training

Day Skipper Shorebased

A perfect precursor to the RYA Intermediate Powerboat course, this is a must for those skippers thinking about cruising further afield or planning to take their boat on holiday. It equips you with enough knowledge to navigate familiar waters by day. A basic knowledge of lights is also included.

Delivered in the classroom or by distance learning, the topics covered include:

- The basics of seamanship
- Chartwork
- Position fixing
- Weather forecasting and meteorology
- Collision regulations
- Construction, parts and equipment of a cruising boat

- Essentials of coastal navigation and pilotage
- Electronic charts
- Plotting a course to steer
- Tides
- Emergency and safety procedures

Your student course pack includes a course handbook, charts, exercises and an electronic chart plotter CD.

How long is the course?

In the classroom, the course is taught over 40 hours, with two assessment papers. Some centres deliver the course as either a series of short sessions, an intensive week-long course, or by distance learning.

Aim: To teach powerboating up to the standard required to complete a short coastal passage by day. The ratio of students to instructors should not exceed 3:1.

Assumed knowledge: Candidates should be competent to the standard of National Powerboat Certificate Level 2 with coastal endorsement. The course may be conducted on a planing or displacement boat.

Knowledge to the level of Day Skipper theory is recommended.

It is strongly recommended that candidates hold a first aid certificate and a VHF/SRC operator's certificate.

Duration: Two days

Minimum age: Sixteen years old

Endorsement: Assistance required to complete the course

Section A: Theory
Planning a Day Cruise
Knowledge of:
- Use of marina locks (can be covered practically if appropriate)

Understands:
- Latitude and longitude
- The principles of GPS and chart plotters
- Sources of forecast information and the interpretation of forecasts
- Tidal heights at secondary ports
- How to use a plotting instrument and plot a course to steer (CTS)
- How to issue distress by all available means

Can:
- Work out tidal heights for standard ports using a tidal curve
- Navigate
- Use true and magnetic bearings
- Interpret bearing and distance
- Interpret chart symbols
- Interpret tidal diamonds and tidal streams
- Use pilot books
- Interpret Lateral and Cardinal buoyage
- Implement IRPCS, in particular rules 5, 6, 7, 8, 9, 12–19, 23
- Use GPS waypoint navigation and determine XTE, SOG, COG, BTW, DTW*
- Use a laminated chart afloat
- Use pilotage to enter an unfamiliar port by day

XTE – Cross Track Error; SOG – Speed Over Ground; COG – Course Over Ground; BTW – Bearing To Waypoint; DTW – Distance To Waypoint

(Continued overleaf)

7 | INTERMEDIATE POWERBOAT DAY CRUISING

Section B: Practical

The aim of the practical session is to put into practice the theory detailed above and to complete a passage, which shall include:

Boat Preparation

Understands:
- The importance of protective clothing and safety equipment
- The minimum level of equipment for the boat
- Considerations of equipment required for longer passages
- Correct stowage of equipment

Boat Handling

Knowledge of:
- Effect of waves
- Rougher conditions
- Awareness of other water users
- Mooring stern-to between posts or Med style

Understands:
- The importance of boat control in waves and adequate seating to minimise the possibility of injury

Can:
- Demonstrate awareness of wind and tide
- Moor alongside, in a marina berth (where available)
- Demonstrate the use of an appropriate length killcord at all times

Pilotage

Can:
- Demonstrate a practical application of techniques for pilotage in local waters

Passage Making

Understands:
- The need for pre-planning, including advice in the event of having to return at night

Can:
- Apply the lessons learnt in the theory section and successfully complete a practical passage
- Fix position by a variety of traditional and electronic means

Man Overboard

Understands:
- Techniques for picking up a man overboard in differing conditions

Can:
- Pick up a man overboard
- Cold shock and immersion hypothermia
- How and when to raise the alarm

Aim: To teach boat handling, seamanship, pilotage and navigation up to the standards required to drive a planing powerboat safely by day and night in tidal coastal waters with which the candidate may be familiar. The course may be conducted on a planing or displacement powerboat with lights conforming to the IRPCS. Students must wear a minimum 150 Newton lifejacket with an MCA-approved light for the night exercise.

Assumed knowledge: Candidates should be competent to the standard of the Intermediate Powerboat Certificate with a thorough knowledge of navigation and chartwork to the level of the Coastal Skipper/RYA Yachtmaster Shorebased certificate.

It is strongly recommended that candidates hold a first aid certificate and a VHF operator's certificate.

Duration: Two days

Minimum age: Seventeen years old

Endorsement: Assistance required to complete the course

Section A: Practical
Preparation for Sea
Can:
- Prepare the powerboat
- Carry out fuel and engine checks
- Stow and secure gear

Boat Handling
Knowledge of:
- Differences for a twin-engine vessel

Understands:
- The importance of boat control in waves and adequate seating to minimise the possibility of injury
- Characteristics of various hull forms and propeller configurations
- Action to be taken in rough weather

Can:
- Demonstrate a practical understanding and correct use of power trim and trim tabs
- Demonstrate an awareness of the effects of wind and tide when manoeuvring, including:
    - Steering to transits and in buoyed channels
    - Turning in a confined space
    - Berthing in various conditions of wind and tide
    - Picking up and leaving a mooring buoy
    - Demonstrate the use of an appropriate length killcord at all times
- Pick up a man overboard in differing conditions

(Continued overleaf)

Passage Making and Responsibility as Skipper

Understands:

* The importance of pre-trip planning
* Planning and making coastal passages, taking into account the relevant navigational hazards, the type of boat and the strengths of the crew
* Chart plotters and radar, their advantages and limitations

Can:

* Organise the navigation, safety and welfare of the crew during a powerboat passage
* Navigate at higher speed using a range of techniques
* Use electronic navigational equipment for planning and undertaking a passage, including the use of waypoints, routes and XTE, SOG, COG, BTW, DTW*

Pilotage

Can:

* Carry out pilotage plans and pilotage for entry into or departure from harbour
* Use leading and clearing lines, transits, back bearings and soundings as aids to pilotage
* Use GPS and understand its limitations in pilotage
* Navigate using soundings

Section B: Theory

Meteorology

Understands:

* Terms used in shipping forecasts, including the Beaufort scale, and their significance to small craft
* Sources of forecast information and interpretation of forecasts including synoptic charts
* The significance of meteorological trends

Can:

* Interpret a synoptic chart
* Use and interpret forecasts to make decisions about passages

Rules of the Road

Can:

Apply the International Regulations for Preventing Collisions at Sea

*XTE – Cross Track Error; SOG – Speed Over Ground; COG – Course Over Ground; BTW – Bearing To Waypoint; DTW – Distance To Waypoint

Use of Engines
Knowledge of:
- How to change a propeller
- Propeller diameter and pitch
- Propeller ventilation and cavitation

Understands:
- Checks to be made before starting, during running, and after stopping for diesel and petrol engines
- Periodic checks on engines and electrical system including spark plugs, water filters and pump impellers
- Transmission belts
- Spares to be carried

Emergency Situations
Understands:
- Correct action to take in emergency situations
- Fire prevention and fighting
- Hull damage/watertight integrity
- What to do in a medical emergency
- Towing and being towed
- Helicopter rescue procedures
- Issue distress by all available means
- Search patterns
- The danger of cold shock and immersion hypothermia

Night Cruising
Can:
- Take charge of a powerboat at night, including leaving and entering harbour
- Demonstrate ability at keeping a proper look-out and identifying lit and unlit positions by night

Coastal Skipper/
RYA Yachtmaster
Offshore Shorebased

For those going cruising coastally and offshore, or with their sights set on the Advanced Powerboat Certificate of Competence exam, this course allows some time for the revision of the basics and then moves on to advanced navigation techniques.

Delivered in the classroom or by distance learning, the topics covered include:

- Position fixing
- Tidal knowledge
- Electronic position finding equipment
- Plotting weather systems
- Collision regulations
- Course shaping and plotting
- Use of almanacs and Admiralty publications
- Taking and interpreting forecasts
- Weather predictions using a barometer and by observation
- Customs & Excise regulations for cruising abroad

Your student course pack includes a course handbook, charts, exercises and an electronic chart plotter CD.

How long is the course?
In the classroom, the course is taught over 40 hours, with three assessment papers. Some centres deliver the course as either a series of short sessions, an intensive week-long course, or by distance learning.

The RYA Advanced Powerboat Examination is a practical test of boat handling and pilotage. It includes an oral and written test on passage planning, chart work, tides, collision regulations, weather and safety. At least some of the test must be undertaken at night.

The previous experience required before taking this examination, and the scope of the syllabus, is shown on the following pages. There is no requirement to attend a course at a training centre before the exam, although many candidates will find it helpful to brush up their skills at a centre. Skippers should ensure that they are familiar with the handling and other characteristics of any vessel they take to sea.

Certificates of Competence are not required in UK waters on board British-flagged pleasure vessels of fewer than 24 metres load line length, or fewer than 80 gross tonnes.

Vessels under 24m in Length used for Sport or Recreation on a Commercial Basis

Vessels used for sport or recreation on a commercial basis are subject to Merchant Shipping legislation. The use of the Advanced Certificate of Competence is permitted for the skippers of these vessels, provided that the certificate has a valid endorsement for commercial use.

To obtain this endorsement, an applicant must obtain a Medical Fitness Certificate, attend a Basic Sea Survival Course, and have an RYA Professional Practices and Responsibilities certificate. Medical Fitness forms, details of the Basic Sea Survival Course and the RYA Professional Practices and Responsibilities online course are available from the RYA or *www.rya.org.uk*.

The endorsement for commercial use is valid for five years. It may be renewed by providing evidence of continuing satisfactory service at sea as skipper or mate of a small commercial vessel, and a Medical Fitness Certificate.

Withdrawal of Certificates

The RYA's Qualification Panel reserves the right to withdraw certificates at any time if due cause is shown.

Own Boat Exams

For the exam, the candidate must provide a seaworthy vessel capable of a minimum of 12 knots, equipped as laid down in the Notes for Candidates, available at *www.rya.org.uk*. The vessel must be efficiently crewed as the examiner will not take part in the management of the vessel during the exam.

All candidates must wear a 150 or 275 Newton lifejacket with a MCA (UK) approved lifejacket light.

Booking an Examination

RYA Advanced Powerboat exams can be booked through our website *www.rya.org.uk*.

Examinations for service personnel are also conducted by the JSASTC, RNSA, RAFSA and ASA. Servicemen should consult the JSASTC or their sailing association for details of examination arrangements.

Exams through a Training Centre

If you take an Advanced course at an RYA Recognised Training Centre, the exam can be arranged through the centre.

(Continued overleaf)

9 | EXAMINATIONS FOR THE RYA/MCA ADVANCED POWERBOAT CERTIFICATE OF COMPETENCE

Exams outside the UK

Overseas examinations must be organised through an RYA Recognised Training Centre which is recognised to run the RYA Advanced Powerboat course. The centre must notify the RYA of any overseas exams and the location must be approved by the RYA.

Exams in New Zealand are organised through CBES:

Coastguard Boating Education Service

165 Westhaven Drive, Westhaven, Auckland 1010, New Zealand

info@boatingeducation.org.nz

Exam Duration

1 candidate 4–5 hours

2 candidates 5–6 hours

3 candidates 6–7 hours

No more than three candidates can be examined in one session.

Pre-exam Requirements

Minimum age: Seventeen years old

Recommended

- RYA Level 2 Powerboat Certificate or equivalent knowledge
- RYA Intermediate Powerboat Certificate or equivalent knowledge
- RYA Coastal Skipper/RYA Yachtmaster shorebased navigation course completion certificate, or equivalent knowledge
- RYA Advanced Powerboat Course Completion Certificate or equivalent knowledge

Minimum seatime required:

- Two years' relevant experience including night pilotage. As a guide 30 days, 2 days as skipper, 800 miles, 12 night hours. If you hold an RYA Advanced Powerboat Course Completion Certificate the seatime is reduced to 20 days, 2 days as skipper, 400 miles, 12 night hours.

Also required:

- A passport photo
- A copy of your VHF/SRC operator's licence
- RYA First Aid Certificate or another acceptable first aid certificate, as detailed on the RYA website.

If you wish to add a commercial endorsement to your certificate you will also need:

- A copy of your Sea Survival certificate
- RYA Professional Practices and Responsibilities Certificate
- A completed ML5 or ENG1 medical report

1 Preparation for Sea
- Preparation of Vessel
- Safety brief
- Stowing and securing gear for coastal passages
- Engine operations and routine checks, fuel systems, killcord
- Fuel system, bleeding, changing filters and impellers

2 Boat Handling
- Hull forms and their handling characteristics, propeller configurations
- Knowledge of action to be taken in rough weather
- Significance of tidal stream on sea conditions
- Steering and power control through waves
- Understanding and correct use of power trim and tabs
- Towing, under open-sea conditions and in confined areas
- Strategy up and downwind and in heavy weather

Awareness of the effects of wind and tide when manoeuvring, including:
- Steering to transits and in buoyed channels
- Turning in a confined space
- All berthing and un-berthing
- Picking up and leaving a mooring buoy
- Anchoring
- Recovery of man overboard
- Awareness of ground speed and ability to hold the boat on station

3 Responsibilities of Skipper
- Skippering the vessel with effective crew communication
- Preparing the vessel for sea and for adverse weather
- Tactics for heavy weather and restricted visibility
- Emergency and distress situations
- Customs procedures
- Courtesy to other water users

4 Passage making and Pilotage
Your chart work and theory knowledge should include:
- Charts, navigational publications and sources of navigational information
- Chart work, including position fixing and shaping course to allow for tide
- Tidal heights and depths
- Buoyage and visual aids to navigation
- Instruments, including compasses, logs, echo sounders, radio navigation aids and chartwork instruments
- Passage planning and navigational tactics
- Understanding the importance of pre-planning

(Continued overleaf)

- Planing-speed navigation, pre-planning and execution
- Use of electronic navigation (GPS & radar)
- Pilotage techniques and plans for entry into or departure from harbour
- Use of leading and clearing lines, transits and soundings as aids to pilotage
- Navigational records
- Limits of navigational accuracy and margins of safety
- Lee shore dangers

You should be able to enter and depart from a charted port by day or night. Your examiner will give you a pilotage exercise and ask you to explain your planning. You will need to be aware of the problems of collision avoidance and how to determine your position by night.

5 Meteorology

You should be able to use weather and tidal information to predict likely sea conditions and make passage planning decisions.

- Definition of terms including the Beaufort scale, and their significance to small craft
- Sources of weather forecasts
- Weather systems and local weather effects
- Interpretation of weather forecasts, barometric trends and visible phenomena
- Ability to make passage planning decisions based on forecast information

6 Rules of the Road

You should be able to apply the International Regulations for Preventing Collisions at Sea. You should be able to identify vessels by day and night.

7 Safety

Candidates will be expected to know what safety equipment should be carried on board the vessel, based either on the recommendations on the RYA website or the Codes of Practice for the Safety of Small Commercial Vessels. In particular, candidates must know the responsibilities of a skipper in relation to:

- Fire prevention and fighting
- Hull damage/watertight integrity
- Medical emergency
- Towing and being towed
- VHF emergency procedures
- Explanation of helicopter rescue procedures
- Use of flares
- Man overboard – recovery methods and associated hazards
- Sector search
- Lifejackets
- Liferafts

Professional Practices and Responsibilities

The Professional Practices and Responsibilities (PPR) course explains the legal framework that you fit into due to your status as a commercial operator. Whatever vessel you work on, it will help you understand and execute your duty of care and give you the principles, guidance and techniques to make the right choices and decisions.

PPR is for anyone using an RYA qualification or Certificate of Competence to gain a commercial endorsement in order to work professionally as skipper or crew.

Whatever your job is on board, you have a duty of care to crew, passengers and other water users. You will be held to account if things go wrong.

Like any other professional industry, commercial boat operations are subject to a vast array of rules, regulations and conventions.

Whether you are a charter skipper, driving a workboat with lifting and towing gear or running a superyacht, this course will help make you aware of the various regulations under which you must operate.

The course is run by RYA Recognised Training Centres through our eLearning site *www.ryainteractive.org.*

There is an instructor on hand to help during the online course and, as you near the end of it, there will be an online assessment.

What you can expect to learn:

- Ensuring your vessel is suitable and legal for the work you are doing
- Creating and implementing risk control and operating procedures
- Compulsory carriage and maintenance of safety equipment
- Your obligations in protecting the environment
- The importance of correct manning
- Your obligations to crew and passengers
- Planning and situational awareness
- The safe management of commercial vessels

The Professional Practices and Responsibilities course is a pre-requisite for anyone applying for or renewing their commercial endorsement through the RYA.

(Continued overleaf)

Sea Survival

A one-day course for anyone going to sea, providing an understanding of how to use the safety equipment on board your boat. A genuine lifesaver.

Powerboating is one of the safest leisure sporting activities, and the vast majority of those afloat will never use their liferaft. However, if you are part of the unlucky few, your chances of survival will be greatly increased if you understand how to use the equipment and how to help yourself.

It is a well-proven fact that, in the event of an emergency at sea, people with training are more likely to survive.

An important part of the course is a practical session in a swimming pool. Experience first-hand the problems of entering an uncooperative liferaft and assisting others while fully kitted out in wet weather gear and a lifejacket.

Course topics include:

- Liferafts and the equipment they contain
- Survival techniques
- The design of lifejackets
- Medical aspects of sea survival
- Search and rescue techniques

Marine Radio (SRC)

A one-day course for anyone who owns a fixed or hand-held marine VHF radio.

The Short Range Certificate is the minimum qualification required by law to control the operation of VHF and VHF Digital Selective Calling (DSC) equipment on any British-flagged vessel voluntarily fitted with a radio. This includes both fixed and hand-held equipment using international channels.

A radio is an important piece of safety equipment on board and it is vital to understand the correct procedures. Unnecessary transmissions could block out a Mayday distress call.

All new VHF sets are either fitted or can be interfaced with DSC, allowing calls to specific vessels. If you hold the 'old' VHF licence (pre-1999) you need to upgrade your qualification if you purchase new equipment. This can be done by attending this one-day course or, if no tuition is required, you can enter for direct examination.

Course topics include:

- The basics of radio operation
- The correct frequencies (channels) to be used
- Distress, emergency and medical assistance procedures
- Making ship-to-shore telephone calls
- Digital Selective Calling (DSC) using simulators
- Global Maritime Distress and Safety System (GMDSS)
- Emergency Position Indicating Radio Beacons (EPIRB)
- Search and Rescue Transponders (SART)

The course will be taught using radio simulators and is examined by a short written test.

(Continued overleaf)

First Aid

Our one-day course covers all the usual first aid subjects, but from a boating perspective. It is aimed at anyone who goes afloat, whether on inland waters, rivers, estuaries or on cross-channel passages.

In a medical emergency a little first aid knowledge and immediate action can save lives, especially in remote locations. This one-day course is designed to support skippers and provide a working knowledge of first aid for people using small craft.

It fulfils the requirements for:

- Professional skippers of small craft working within 60 miles of a safe haven, including Boatmasters
- The Senior First Aid certificate needed by offshore racers subject to World Sailing regulations on first aid training (OSR 4.08.4)

The course is recommended by the MCA and HSE.

The subjects specific to boating include:

- The recovery position in a confined space
- CPR, including the drowning protocol
- Cold shock and hypothermia from immersion and/or exposure
- Seasickness and dehydration
- Medical assistance or advice by VHF
- Helicopter rescue

Year	Boat details	Hours as Driver	Details of passage, weather, distance covered
Oct 2019	PB Course RHIBS	6	0 - Force 5 wind. S. Cyprus

13 | LOGBOOK

Year	Boat details	Hours as Driver	Details of passage, weather, distance covered

Year	Boat details	Hours as Driver	Details of passage, weather, distance covered

13 | LOGBOOK

Year	Boat details	Hours as Driver	Details of passage, weather, distance covered

Year	Boat details	Hours as Driver	Details of passage, weather, distance covered

POWERBOAT INSTRUCTOR SKILLS ASSESSMENT

Date: _____   Inland or Coastal: _____

Centre: _____   Trainer: _____

13 | RECOMMENDED READING

The aim of this logbook is to introduce you to the sport of powerboating and help you gain competence and confidence.

By now, you will probably want to learn more – about engines, boat handling and navigation. Libraries and chandlers are full of books on boating, but the ones below are particularly recommended.

RYA Start Powerboating
ISBN: 978-1-906435479
RYA Order Code: G48

For courses:
Level 1 Start
Powerboating;
Level 2
Powerboat
Handling.

RYA Powerboat Handbook
ISBN: 978-1-910017029
RYA Order Code: G13

For course:
RYA Intermediate
Powerboat Day
Cruising.

RYA Safety Boat Handbook
ISBN: 978-1-905104383
RYA Order Code: G16

For course:
Safety Boat Course.

RYA Advanced Powerboat Handbook
ISBN: 978-1-906435981
RYA Order Code: G108

For course:
Advanced
Powerboat
Day & Night.

RYA Navigation Handbook
ISBN: 978-1-906435943
RYA Order Code: G6

For courses:
RYA Intermediate
Powerboat Day
Cruising;
Advanced
Powerboat
Day & Night.

RYA Navigation Exercises
ISBN: 978-1-905104185
RYA Order Code: G7

For courses:
RYA Intermediate
Powerboat Day
Cruising;
Advanced
Powerboat
Day & Night.

A Seaman's Guide to the Rule of the Road
ISBN: 978-0-948254581
RYA Order Code: ZS09

For courses: RYA Intermediate
Powerboat Day Cruising;
Advanced Powerboat Day & Night.

RYA Weather Handbook
ISBN: 978-1-910017142
RYA Order Code: G133

For courses:
RYA Intermediate
Powerboat Day
Cruising;
Advanced
Powerboat
Day & Night.

RYA An Introduction to Radar
ISBN: 978-1-905104109
RYA Order Code: G34

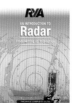

For:
RYA/MCA
Advanced
Powerboat
Certificate of
Competence.

Shop online at
www.rya.org.uk/shop

- Secure online ordering
- 15% discount for RYA members
- Books, DVDs, navigation aids and lots more
- Free delivery to a UK address for RYA members on orders over £25
- Free delivery to an overseas address for RYA members on orders over £50
- Buying online from the RYA shop enables the RYA in its work on behalf of its members

RYA